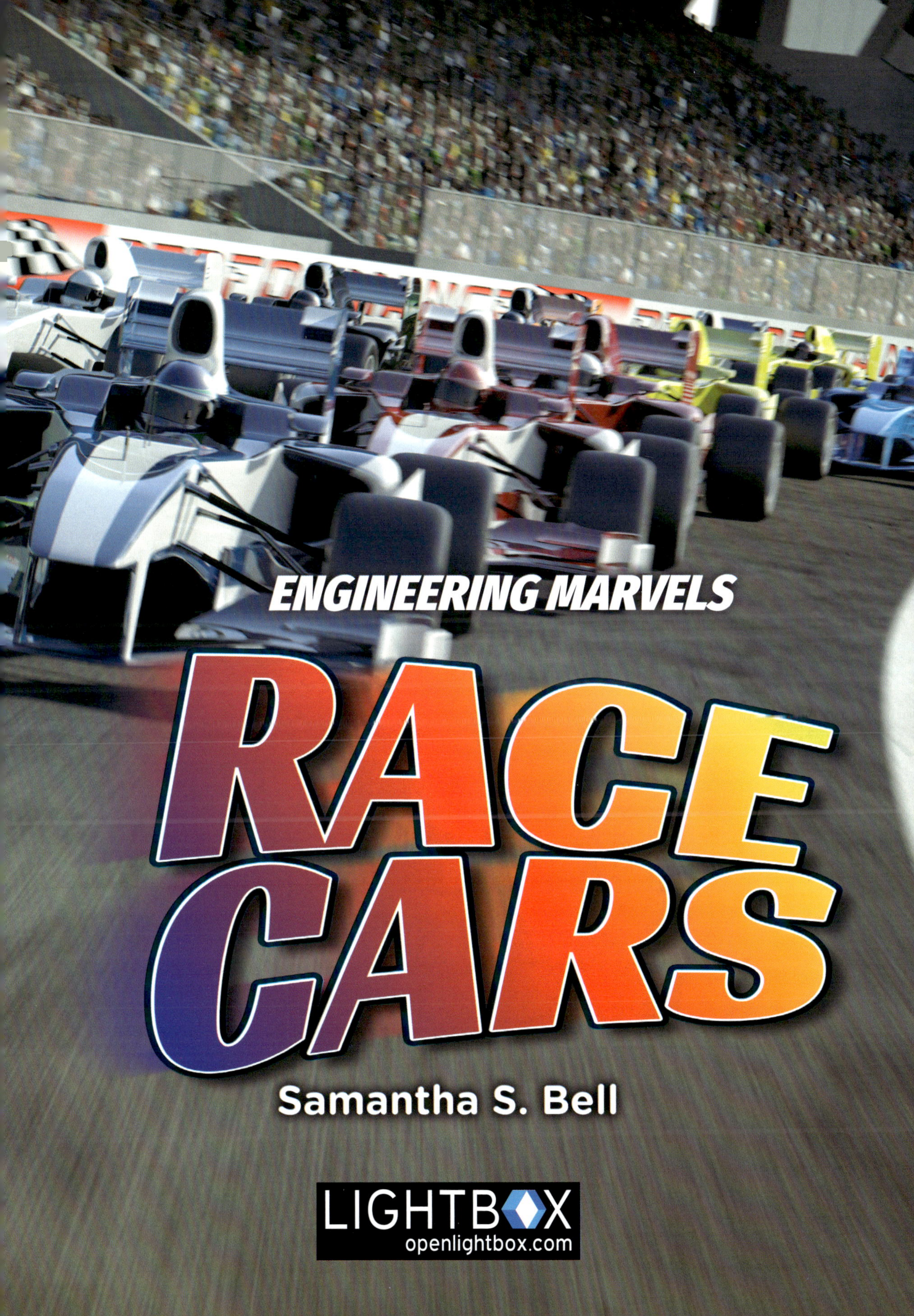

ENGINEERING MARVELS

RACE CARS

Samantha S. Bell

LIGHTBOX
openlightbox.com

Lightbox is an all-inclusive digital solution for the teaching and learning of curriculum topics in an original, groundbreaking way. Lightbox is based on National Curriculum Standards.

STANDARD FEATURES OF LIGHTBOX

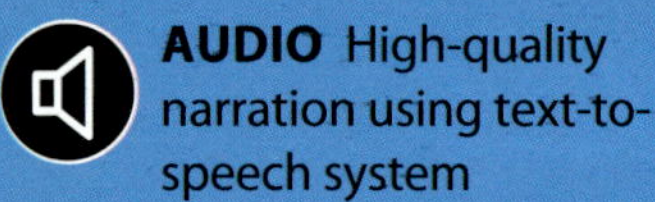
AUDIO High-quality narration using text-to-speech system

ACTIVITIES Printable PDFs that can be emailed and graded

SLIDESHOWS Pictorial overviews of key concepts

VIDEOS Embedded high-definition video clips

WEBLINKS Curated links to external, child-safe resources

TRANSPARENCIES Step-by-step layering of maps, diagrams, charts, and timelines

INTERACTIVE MAPS Interactive maps and aerial satellite imagery

QUIZZES Ten multiple choice questions that are automatically graded and emailed for teacher assessment

KEY WORDS Matching key concepts to their definitions

Contents

Chapter 1

Racing from the Start

The first gasoline-powered automobile was built around 1885. Ten years later, in 1895, Émile Levassor became the first car racing champion. The course was more than 700 miles (1,127 kilometers) across France. Levassor averaged only 15 miles per hour (24 km/h). And he finished in just under 49 hours.

The first race cars were often driven by the same people who built them.

Much has changed since that 1895 race. But cars and racing are still very much connected. Race cars are automobiles specifically designed for speed. Drivers compete in races around the world to see who is the fastest. Today's cars can go faster than 200 miles per hour (322 km/h). Yet all are designed to keep the drivers as safe as possible.

The car industry was still new in the early 1900s. Racing proved to be a good way for companies to show off their new cars. Henry Ford used a race car in 1902 to show off his design skills. He went on to start what is now the Ford Motor Company. Race cars have long had the best available technology. Many new features were first demonstrated at racetracks.

In the 1920s, people began racing their personal cars. These are called stock cars. But auto racing came to a halt during World War II (1939–1945). Cars were only produced for the war effort.

Race cars of the early 1900s went about 70 miles per hour (110 km/h).

The **first auto race** held after World War II was in Paris, France. It had **200,000** spectators.

Indianapolis Motor Speedway is a well-known racetrack. It opened in **1909**.

Stock car racing became popular in the 1930s. Cars raced down **4.2 miles** (6.7 km) of beach in Daytona, Florida.

Since the 1990s, stock car racing has become very popular. It is the second-most watched sport on television, behind major league football.

Racing began again after the war ended. Race organizers created the National Association for Stock Car Auto Racing (NASCAR). This group organized stock car racing on oval tracks throughout the southern United States.

After World War II, the fastest European race cars became known as Formula One cars. On these cars, the wheels are exposed with no **fenders**. This is called open wheel. Their races were mostly on closed-off roads. The fastest open-wheel cars in the United States were called IndyCars. They were known for racing the Indianapolis 500. It began in 1911 at Indianapolis Motor Speedway.

Today, Formula One cars race all over the world. These cars race on special racetracks. NASCAR races are held at tracks in North America. IndyCars race on many of these same tracks. However, stock cars and IndyCars never compete in the same races.

Chapter 2

Fast and Faster

Engineers design different types of cars depending on the racing style. Stock cars have the same body shape as the cars we see on the road.

However, stock cars have added features for both speed and protection. Formula One and IndyCars are single-seat cars. Their wheels are outside of the main body. Their engines are in the rear.

Companies pay millions of dollars to put their logos on IndyCars.

Racing leagues set basic guidelines for the cars. Each car must meet a minimum weight, maximum engine size, maximum width, and minimum height.

As a car moves, high-pressure air pushes on it from the front. The car must push the air out of the way. Meanwhile, the path the air takes as it goes over the car can create lift. This is a force that can pull the car off the ground. Therefore, engineers create **aerodynamic** designs in an effort to reduce the **drag** and increase the **downforce**.

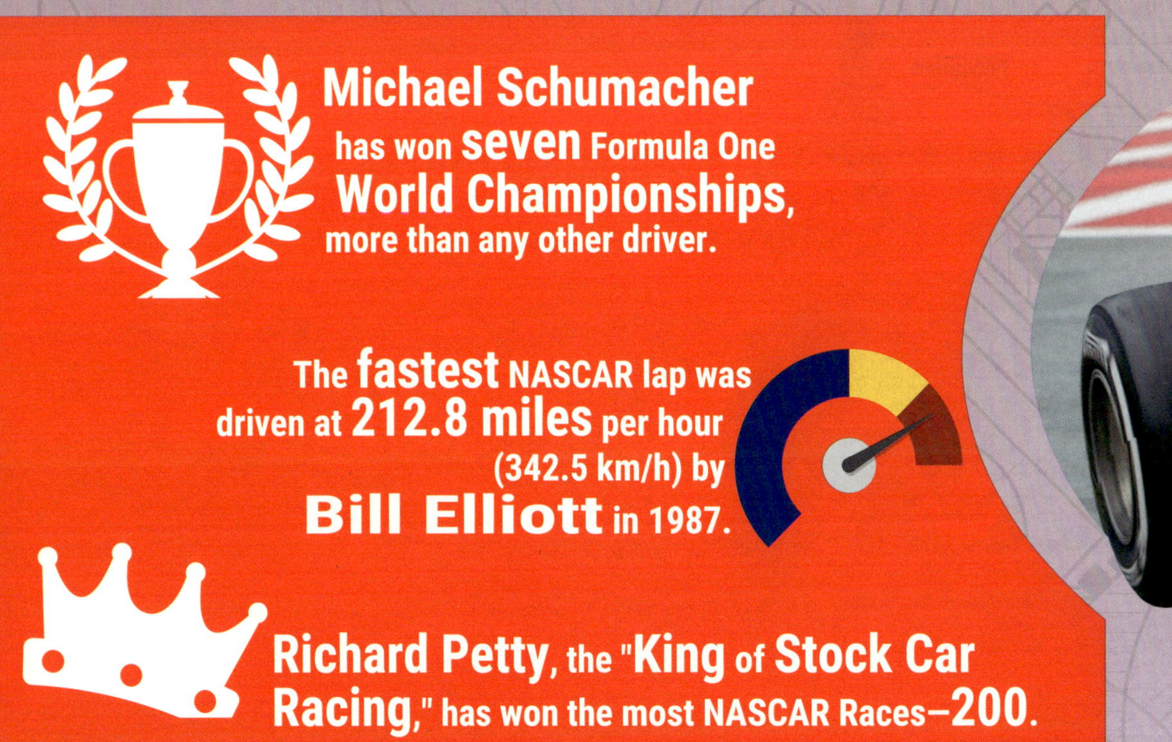

Added downforce increases the ground pressure and therefore the grip. Grip is also called traction. Increased traction improves both **acceleration** and **cornering** speed. Traction comes from the force the tire applies against the ground. Most racing tires are completely smooth. Each tire's entire surface can touch the track, giving the tires better grip.

Some parts of a Formula One car are only 2 inches (5 centimeters) off the ground.

Formula One and IndyCars are faster than stock cars. These cars have a smaller frontal area. It is the part of the car that pushes through the air. This makes the cars more aerodynamic. A rear engine allows the driver to sit lower in the car. Because of the lower **center of gravity**, the driver can go faster around corners without the car's wheels lifting. This keeps the car from rolling over.

Rear-engine cars also have better traction. Having more engine weight in the rear increases the ground pressure on the back wheels. This means more power can be used for acceleration and cornering before the back tires lose grip.

Engineers have options for improving their cars. For example, they can increase acceleration by reducing weight, increasing power, or both. In addition, some rules allow for special parts or designs to be added to cars. Some cars can have upside-down wings at the front or back. These wings create downforce.

The Daytona 500 is NASCAR's most important race.

Designers can also shape the car to create a **vacuum** effect under the car. This also increases downforce. The spoiler attached to the front of stock cars can also cause this vacuum.

Engineers also add safety features to protect drivers. These can include harnesses, **fuel cells**, removable seats, padding, and head and neck restraints.

NASCAR requires safety equipment, such as fire extinguishers, window netting, and roll cages, in each car.

Engineering Design Process

Engineers use many tools and computer programs in their planning. Once a race car is built, engineers perform many tests in the shop and on the track to prove that the design meets their expectations.

ASK What type of race will the car compete in? How can the car's acceleration and cornering speed be improved? How can the car be made more aerodynamic? What can be added to protect the driver?

IMAGINE Brainstorm possible car designs. What design would give the car the fastest acceleration?

PLAN Draw a diagram of the car. Make a list of materials needed. Write down a list of steps.

CREATE Follow the plan and build a race car.

IMPROVE What worked with the car? What did not work? Change your design to make the car faster.

Chapter 3

The Ford GT

In 2016, Ford entered its new GT in the Rolex 24 race in Daytona, Florida. The car had many advanced features. The aerodynamic design produced more downforce for faster cornering, better stability, and less drag. The car had a strong, light **chassis** and a powerful new V6 engine.

The Ford GT is a favorite for endurance races, which last for six hours or longer.

The Rolex 24 is a 24-hour race. Ford entered the No. 66 and No. 67 cars. But just 16 minutes in, No. 67 began having trouble. The car lost speed and would not shift correctly. It had to be taken to the garage to be fixed. Then the car had more problems. A diffuser, used to help create vacuum downforce, was damaged. It rubbed against one of the car's tires, cutting it two times. Crews had to replace part of the car's transmission. No. 66 had transmission problems, too. Soon both cars were too far behind to catch up.

Ford had expected to win the race with one of the cars. Neither ended in the top five of its class. But the team learned a lot about the new GT. And they knew what they needed to fix for next time.

At the 2017 Rolex 24 race, car No. 66's best lap was at 123.7 miles per hour (199.1 km/h).

Ford entered the cars into the 2017 Rolex 24 race. No. 66 often took the lead during the first few hours. Cold and wet weather conditions made the nighttime driving difficult, but No. 66 pushed to the front again and again. The GT finished first in its category and fifth overall.

Chapter 4

Ferrari SF70H driver Sebastian Vettel has won four Formula One World Championships.

The Ferrari SF70H

Formula One cars must follow certain rules in their designs. In 2017, some major changes were made in the rules. The car bodies and tires had to be wider. This improved downforce and traction. The rear wings also had to be wider and lower.

Ferrari did not win a single race in 2016. So in 2017, engineers used the new rules to build a better car. They created the Ferrari SF70H. It had a sharply angled front and a longer nose. This made it more aerodynamic. Designers also added a shark fin to the engine cover. It helped move air away from the new rear wing, especially while the car was going around corners.

The car did well in practice, but the true test was on the track. The new design was a success! In the opening race of the 2017 season, the Ferrari SF70H won by nearly 10 seconds.

Mapping Race Tracks

The United States is home to some of the best-known auto racing in the world. Drivers make and break world records in their fine-tuned race cars every year. The map shows where some of these engineering marvels race. Are there any race tracks near where you live?

Atlanta Motor Speedway

Hampton, Georgia

The largest sporting events in Georgia—two NASCAR Nextel Cup Series races—are held on the Atlanta Motor Speedway. The 1.5-mile (2.4-km) track opened in 1960 with seats for 71,000 spectators.

Talladega Superspeedway

Talladega, Alabama

The Talladega Superspeedway has been the site of many records in stock car racing, including Bill Elliot's fastest lap in 1987. The $4-million track opened in 1969 and seats 143,000 fans.

Circuit of the Americas

Austin, Texas

The 3.4-mile (5.5-km) Circuit of the Americas opened in 2012. It is home to Formula One races held in the United States and has seated as many as 120,000 spectators.

UNITED STATES

1

3

2

Atlantic Ocean

Pacific Ocean

Hawai'i

100 Miles

0 161 Kilometers

Alaska

500 Miles

0 804 Kilometers

Legend

Water

Land

United States

N W E S

250 Miles

0 402 Kilometers

Timeline

Auto racing in the United States started more than 100 years ago. Today, it remains a popular sport, with millions of fans across the country. Discover more about the history of racing in the United States.

1895

The first organized car race in the United States runs 54 miles (87 km) between Chicago and Evanston, Illinois.

1948

The first NASCAR race is held on the beach in Florida. Close to 14,000 spectators paid $2.50 each to watch the historic race.

1979

The Daytona 500 is aired on television. It is the first 500-mile (800-km) race to be aired from start to finish.

2005

An average of 9 million people watch each NASCAR race aired on television.

2008

Danica Patrick of Wisconsin wins the Indy Japan 300 in Motegi, Japan. She is the first woman to win an IndyCar race.

2017

Scott Dixon sets the fastest lap of the Indianapolis 500 during qualifications with a speed of 232.2 miles per hour (373.7 km/h).

Build a Race Car

Engineers build super fast race cars with top-of-the-line equipment. Use household products to make your own!

Materials

Use a toilet paper tube, two straws, and four spools with or without thread to make your car. Masking tape, a pen, and a ruler can help put everything together.

Procedure

1. With a ruler, draw a straight line from one opening of the toilet paper tube to the other. Measure 1 inch (2.5 cm) from one end. Mark this spot on your line as "#1." Then measure 1 inch from the other side. Mark this spot on the line as "#2."

2. Turn the toilet paper tube so the openings are to the side. Place the end of the ruler at #1. Roll the tube. Make a mark 2 inches (5 cm) away. Label this mark "#3." Then do the same from #2. Label this one "#4."

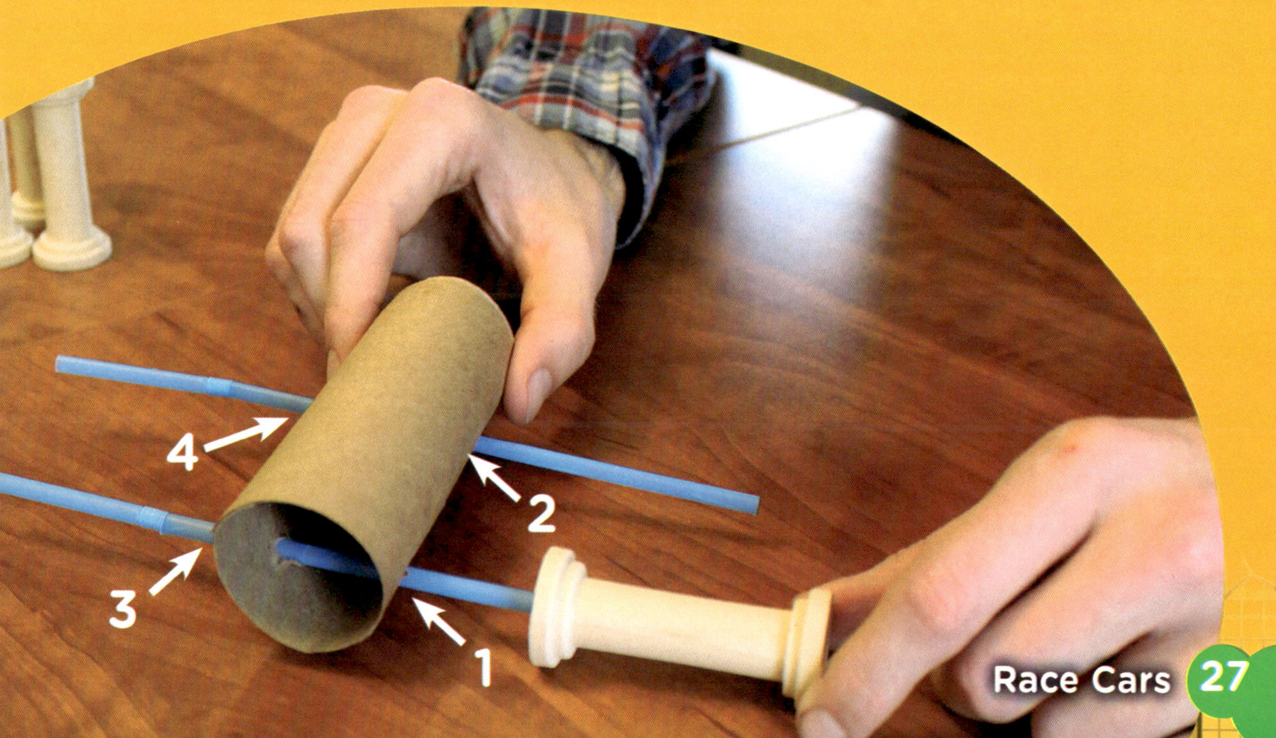

3. Use the tip of your pen to punch holes in the tube at each of the four marks.

4. Push a straw through mark #1 and mark #3. The straw should stick out from the sides of the tube. Push another straw through mark #2 and #4.

5. Remove any labels from the spools. Slide one spool onto each of the four straws. To secure the spools, add a piece of masking tape to the end of each straw.

6. Test your race car! Try rolling it on a smooth surface, such as a table.

Improve It!

The car is shaped like a cylinder. How can you change its shape to make it more aerodynamic?

Quiz

1. When was the first gasoline-powered automobile built?

2. How fast did race cars of the early 1900s go?

3. Stock car races are held on tracks that are what shape?

4. Which race cars look like cars seen on the road?

5. What is the force that can pull a car off the ground?

6. Who has won the most NASCAR races?

7. Are Formula One cars and IndyCars single-seat or double-seat?

8. Does a vacuum effect under the car increase or decrease downforce?

9. Where are Formula One races held in the United States?

10. Who was the first woman to win an IndyCar race?

Answers

1. Around 1885 **2.** About 70 miles per hour (110 km/h) **3.** Oval
4. Stock cars **5.** Lift **6.** Richard Petty **7.** Single-seat **8.** Increase
9. Circuit of the Americas in Austin, Texas **10.** Danica Patrick

Key Words

acceleration: the process of moving faster

aerodynamic: the quality of an object that affects how easily it is able to move through the air

center of gravity: the average center of all of an object's weight

chassis: the frame of a motor vehicle

cornering: driving around a sharp curve

downforce: a force produced by air resistance that pushes down on a vehicle

drag: a force that opposes motion, usually air resistance or rolling friction

fenders: guards that cover a car's wheels

fuel cells: rubber sacs inside a fuel tank that limit leakage if the fuel tank is punctured

vacuum: a space without air

Index

LIGHTBOX

SUPPLEMENTARY RESOURCES

Click on the plus icon found in the bottom left corner of each spread to open additional teacher resources.

- Download and print the book's quizzes and activities
- Access curriculum correlations
- Explore additional web applications that enhance the Lightbox experience

LIGHTBOX DIGITAL TITLES

Packed full of integrated media

VIDEOS

INTERACTIVE MAPS

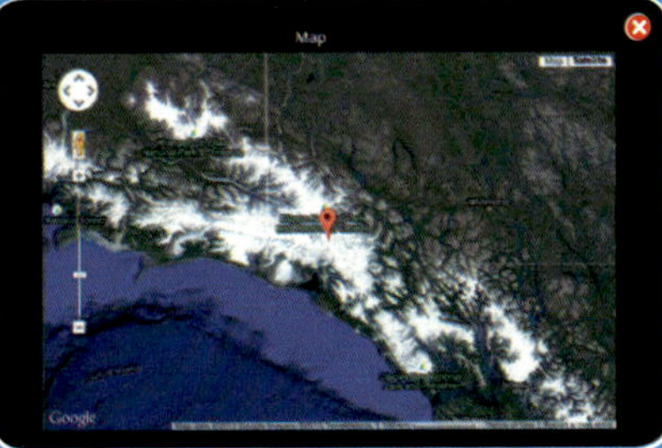

WEBLINKS

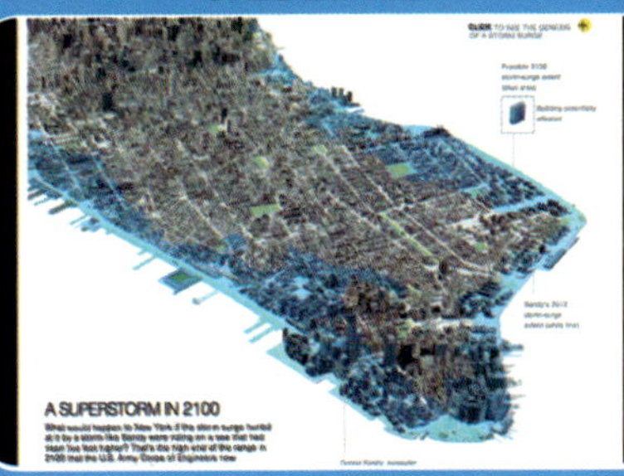

SLIDESHOWS

QUIZZES

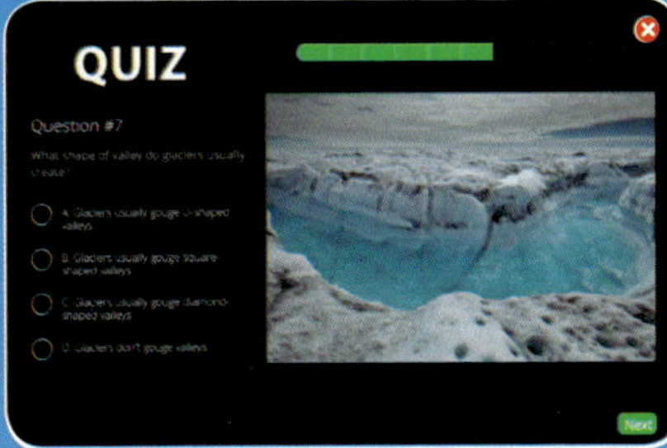

OPTIMIZED FOR

- ✓ TABLETS
- ✓ WHITEBOARDS
- ✓ COMPUTERS
- ✓ AND MUCH MORE!

Published by Smartbook Media Inc.
350 5th Avenue, 59th Floor New York, NY 10118
Website: www.openlightbox.com

012018
151217

Library of Congress Control Number: 2017961992

ISBN 978-1-5105-3732-3 (hardcover)
ISBN 978-1-5105-3733-0 (multi-user eBook)

Printed in the Brainerd, Minnesota, United States
1 2 3 4 5 6 7 8 9 0 22 21 20 19 18

First published by North Star Editions in 2018.

Project Coordinator: Jared Siemens
Designer: Ana María Vidal

Every reasonable effort has been made to trace ownership and to obtain permission to reprint copyright material. The publisher would be pleased to have any errors or omissions brought to its attention so that they may be corrected in subsequent printings.

The publisher acknowledges Alamy, Newscom, Getty Images, iStock, and Shutterstock as the primary image suppliers for this title.